QuoteOctopus.com

The best quotes

Publisher Contact

257 Swanston Street, Melbourne, VIC, AUSTRALIA

Email: hello@quoteoctopus.com

Social media: facebook.com/quoteoctopus

Acknowledgements

The team at Quote Octopus would like to thank our friends, family, suppliers and customers for making our vision of creating the highest-quality books a reality. Thanks for purchasing and enjoy the quotes!

This page is intentionally left blank

This page is intentionally left blank

'Blazing Saddles' is one of the funniest movies ever made.

Adam McKay

'Firewall' seems both scary and protective at the same time. And how often does that happen within one word besides 'military' and 'government?'

Adam McKay

'Step Brothers 2' would have been fun, there's no doubt about it. Maybe someday. Does that idea age? I don't know. It all depends on how the movie ages.

Adam McKay

'The Real World' is the most predictable arc ever. They get on the show, they're all excited, we're gonna be best friends, then people start drinking and get hammered, and say stupid stuff, and that's pretty much it.

Adam McKay

A dry stretch of commentary in the middle of an 'Anchorman' movie would have been a terrible thing.

Adam McKay

A lot of shorts spend too much time setting up the idea; sometimes they meander.

Adam McKay

Actually, 'Wayne's World 2' I kind of liked. I think 'Wayne's World 2' does have some creative things in it, some ideas in it.

Adam McKay

After thousands of hours of news coverage, we have learned that Hillary is a liar and Barack is a terrorist or something.

Adam McKay

All we have is our vote. But it's powerful.

Adam McKay

All you can really do as director is sort of set a tone.

Adam McKay

America is a country that prides itself on being able to identify a 'straight shooter' or 'the genuine article' when it comes to our leaders. As a nation, we can 'feel it in our gut' when someone is giving us a bum steer.

Adam McKay

Any time Chris Nolan wants to call me for advice, he can.

Adam McKay

Anyone in the comedy world knows that Horatio Sanz and Chris Parnell are two of the funniest guys around.

Adam McKay

Arnold Schwarzenegger cut teacher's salaries and parks and libraries rather than raise taxes for the many California millionaires and billionaires.

Adam McKay

As far as how much you listen to the audience, you listen to them when they really hate something.

Adam McKay

As far as what makes a viral video, then it's gotta be something that you've either never seen before, a fresh piece of comedy, or something that relates to something topical.

Adam McKay

Basically, we used to have a rule at 'Saturday Night Live' that you're not allowed to bring up 'The Simpsons' at the rewrite table, because 'The Simpsons' has done every joke there is. Every week there would be guys going, 'The Simpsons did that.' I go, 'C'mon.' And 'South Park,' too.

Adam McKay

Benito Mussolini created the word 'fascism.' He defined it as 'the merging of the state and the corporation.' He also said a more accurate word would be 'corporatism.' This was the definition in Webster's up until 1987 when a corporation bought Webster's and changed it to exclude any mention of corporations.

Adam McKay

Billions have been spent for one purpose and one purpose only: to obscure and distract from the fact that Mitt Romney is backing the identical agenda George W. Bush did.

Adam McKay

Bush already gave obscene tax breaks to people like me and Warren Buffet, and we are saying it's not fair.

Adam McKay

Can anything good come of a backward way of thinking like judging someone based on skin color? No way.

Adam McKay

Celebrities and 'famous' people are just regular folks. I know, it's a shocking and potentially dangerous statement.

Adam McKay

Creative freedom is a huge carrot.

Adam McKay

Dave Herman as Michael Bolton is one of my favorite performances ever.

Adam McKay

David O. Russell is probably my favorite filmmaker. He's not only a great director, but he's also a great writer.

Adam McKay

Depending on what state you live in, you may only have right-wing talk radio and FOX or CBN with MSNBC three hundred channels down the dial.

Adam McKay

Dick Cheney and Bush's rise to power were built on tons of money from corporations and a dulled press.

Adam McKay

Every time a congressman or pundit says its 'class warfare' to increase taxes on the wealthy, it's a massive lie.

Adam McKay

Every time a pundit or elected official is on any TV news program, it should be a polite formality to mention that GE has made such and such billions off the war in Iraq by selling arms or that Murdoch is a right-wing activist with a clear stake in who wins and who taxes his profits the least.

Adam McKay

Everything in America is so stratified by class now. We have the 93rd level of income inequality in the world. You're already seeing highway lanes that are for pay and ones that aren't.

Adam McKay

First and foremost when you're doing comedy, you gotta be relevant and applicable to the times that you're living in. When you try and just do comedy about who is dating who and lifestyle jokes, it gets tiring after a while. It's hard to be funny in that realm.

Adam McKay

First off, no one award-wise ever rewards comedy, which is... whatever. I don't care about that.

Adam McKay

For 'Breaking Bad,' people were with Walter White for 99% of that show, even though that guy is a monster.

Adam McKay

For my money, I don't think there's been a better comedy than 'Kung Fu Hustle' in a lot of years. That movie just knocked me over.

Adam McKay

For some reason, people with comedy, any time they can detect a pattern, it kind of freaks them out. 'Those guys are always together!' Yeah, they're a comedy team. Anything they can recognize as a pattern they think is a hole.

Adam McKay

Friends give me a hard time about the pants I'm wearing, which are made in China. Well, how do you find the right clothes? Or the right movie studio? The right people giving you checks? Good luck doing the right thing all the time.

Adam McKay

George W. Bush was a silver spoon dolt with no record to speak of other than bankruptcy and selling tropical plants, and we let him sail into the White House, but Barack talks about religious fundamentalism and guns being prevalent in poor areas, and we roast him for weeks?

Adam McKay

Governor Palin leans far closer to 'spokesperson' than representative of the people.

Adam McKay

Having a guy on a microphone yelling lines at you is counter to a lot of acting techniques.

Adam McKay

Having two kids, I don't get out to see stand up much anymore.

Adam McKay

I actually opened for Chris Rock at the Funny Bone one time.

Adam McKay

I always say the classier cousin of 'Anchorman' is 'Mad Men,' because when you really look at it, why do people really love Don Draper in 'Mad Men?' He's just a terrible guy. But we know why he's terrible, and I think that's really key to why you can be sympathetic to a character.

Adam McKay

I always thought George Bush was more oblivious than mean, but oblivious can quickly go to mean.

Adam McKay

I am actually talking about possibly adapting 'The Boys,' by Garth Ennis, which would not be a comedy, but an action movie with comedy elements to it.

Adam McKay

I can't exactly say why there's not much protest music to speak off. And I know there are acts out there still putting a message in their music.

Adam McKay

I do have to give it up for Sarah Palin on one account. She is brave.

Adam McKay

I don't think arrested-adolescent humor will fade. Maybe the form will change, but I guarantee its replacement will still be based in immature behavior from mature figures.

Adam McKay

I don't want to speak for my movies; you could say my movies are just completely silly and dumb, but in the case of 'Idiocracy' and 'Borat,' without a doubt there is a really subversive and sophisticated assault on American culture.

Adam McKay

I got the sense that Alabama is a place where people don't want handouts and don't much care for people talking out of the side of their mouth.

Adam McKay

I gotta say - if I clicked on a movie interview, and the first part was all about Walt Whitman, I'd love that article.

Adam McKay

I guess HBO did a giant 'War in the Pacific' mini-series that cost, like, a fortune, and there was a little moment where they literally had no money. And even though the show had become kind of a cult hit, there was an issue of whether they could actually afford to do it.

Adam McKay

I have no political ax to grind; I just find it absurd that huge billion-dollar corporations can take over elections. I just find it insane that, for instance, we give tax breaks to people like myself making millions of dollars, while there're no tax breaks for working people. That, to me, is not a political issue, that's a life issue.

Adam McKay

I have no tax breaks or corporate interests to be supported by Barack Obama.

Adam McKay

I hired Tina Fey for 'SNL,' which was certainly a good match. She took off right away there.

Adam McKay

I hired a personal trainer to help me lose 25 pounds and get from obese to fat. My next step will be to get from fat to chubby.

Adam McKay

I like to remind myself how hard acting is. I do parts in friends' stuff.

Adam McKay

I love 'The Wire;' that's my favorite show, so I'll watch that.

Adam McKay

I love Paul Rudd.

Adam McKay

I love action movies.

Adam McKay

I think everyone knows the news has become ridiculous. It's entertainment driven.

Adam McKay

I think there's a tendency to think geeks and nerds are just sweet guys that were picked on, but that hasn't been my experience. I'm certainly not like that, in a lot of ways.

Adam McKay

I think when a lot of actors hear improv, they think of throwing a line in or doing a slightly different take.

Adam McKay

I want to see Brian Williams with no irony wearing a mustache.

Adam McKay

I was a huge fan of comedy in high school.

Adam McKay

I was born in Colorado and grew up in Pennsylvania with family in Texas and Oklahoma.

Adam McKay

I was completely with the reality TV boom for a while. I really liked a lot of the reality TV, and the one that lost me was the ballroom dancing one they do, 'Dancing with the Stars.' That was the one where I watched it and I was perplexed. I thought it was really boring.

Adam McKay

I was shocked when 'The Hobbit' ended where it ended. I wasn't paying attention to what they were doing; I didn't know they had another movie, and I couldn't believe it was when the dragon came out.

Adam McKay

I would never do 'Stardust Memories' because I don't particularly like that kind of movie - that would be why I wouldn't do that.

Adam McKay

I'll tell you one thing... no doubt about it, my favorite kind of comedy is talking head comedy. I mean, if it were up to me, I'd do a whole entire movie that was just around a dinner table.

Adam McKay

I'm a huge hip hop fan going way back, like, back to '83. I had my Gemini mixer listening to Run-DMC and Kurtis Blow.

Adam McKay

I'm sure when they partied when Rome was burning, that was a really great party.

Adam McKay

If someone busted into your house and robbed you, would you then forgive them if you found out they were a veteran? Of course not. So why are we forgiving McCain for selling out his country by supporting the Bush agenda?

Adam McKay

If you aim for parody right off the bat and it misses, no offense to the filmmakers, but it is Meet the Spartans.

Adam McKay

If you do a Western that's funny, there's no way people don't call it a spoof or a parody, even though it may not be.

Adam McKay

If you go back and watch 'The French Connection,' it's been cannibalized so many times. There are certain movies like that, where you see the original and think, 'This isn't so great.' And the reason it isn't so great is because everyone has copied it.

Adam McKay

If you look at 'Avatar,' could you imagine if you did 'Avatar' for 50 million dollars? It would be ridiculous! You would almost be getting laughs from the audience, unless you got a real indie director to do something incredibly stylised.

Adam McKay

If you make action movies, the critics will savage you, and then your movies are outdated the following week with the new wave of special effects.

Adam McKay

If you're calling yourself a maverick and you're not Dirk Nowitzki, then you are probably not one. In fact, this rule applies to anyone declaring themselves a 'God-fearing Christian' or a 'Man of the people.'

Adam McKay

If you're making comedies, they have to have a fun and a rhythm to them.

Adam McKay

In the past, in the '60s and '70s, genres were much more segmented. You had action guys who were deadly serious about it, and I think you had comics that were comics.

Adam McKay

It should be a law for one whole year that all laugh tracks are Seth Rogen. The world would get ever so slightly better.

Adam McKay

It's Will Ferrell, he does Will Ferrell movies. But if you really look at it, he tries to do something different with each one, whether it's an action cop movie like 'The Other Guys' or doing 'Talladega Nights' going into red state America or 'Casa de Mi Padre' or 'Stranger Than Fiction,' which is more of a drama.

Adam McKay

It's just funny that Americans have to contend with 2000 channels, and 60 different specific news sources, and the confusion that it creates, and the junk that we get to see is hilarious.

Adam McKay

It's one thing to break stuff and damage people's possessions, but when you start aiming at the ideology of America, that's dangerous comedy.

Adam McKay

It's time Hawaii answer doubters and produce documents proving that it is a state. What are they hiding? And why haven't we seen these documents?

Adam McKay

Matt Braunger really makes me laugh; I like that guy a lot.

Adam McKay

McCain is the kid who was really cool in middle school but never got high school game and people are sick of him acting like he's still popular.

Adam McKay

Michael Lewis has the amazing ability to take complex formulas and concepts and turn them into page-turners.

Adam McKay

My first joke was about a company called Five Star Parking that was all over Philadelphia: 'Who's reviewing parking lots?'

Adam McKay

My theme song is 'One Tin Soldier' by Coven.

Adam McKay

My wife is pretty geeky and will occasionally quote 'Anchorman' at me.

Adam McKay

Nothing heightens chaos more than a berserk wild animal right in the middle.

Adam McKay

Nothing is funnier than confidently doing the wrong thing.

Adam McKay

Nothing is more enjoyable for me than when I'm watching a movie or a TV show and there's that sense that anything can happen. It is the most fun feeling in the world.

Adam McKay

Nowadays, the truth is, I think a lot of the newer generation of action stars usually are pretty self-deprecating and cool. I mean, Dwayne Johnson is a great example.

Adam McKay

Obama is the new kid with the weird name who people just sense is a little classier than his surroundings. He moved from a private school where he was class president and is now at the giant public high school with the metal detectors and the smoking lounge.

Adam McKay

Obamacare is a private mandate that will drive billions to the insurance industry, much like the auto insurance mandate. Hardly socialism. In fact, it was a Republican plan to begin with.

Adam McKay

Other than Green Day, we haven't had a lot of protest music over the past few decades.

Adam McKay

Pete Wilson deregulated energy as a pay out to Enron, and we blamed Gray Davis.

Adam McKay

Sequels are desperate.

Adam McKay

Since FDR's New Deal, corporations and wealthy families have been non-stop finding new ways to get tax breaks, deregulation and entitlements from the government.

Adam McKay

Sometimes I know a joke I'm going to yell out ahead of time, but most of the time it's stream of conscious. You never really know it until you've got everyone dressed up, the set is built, all the extras are here.

Adam McKay

Sony is the coolest studio. They are really amazing. I think part of it comes from they're not an American corporation. They don't work by quite the same rules. And their studio heads have a lot of autonomy.

Adam McKay

That's always the trick with the sequels, is how much do you repeat from the first one. Because we all get bummed out when you go see a sequel and it's beat for beat.

Adam McKay

The 'Police Academy' stuff was all hyper-slapsticky.

Adam McKay

The corporate right fires up the religious right against gay marriage and abortion and uses their votes to push their deregulation and tax cuts for the rich. It's an old trick. The House of Saud has the same arrangement with the Mullahs in Saudi Arabia.

Adam McKay

The crush of lobbyists on Washington and purchase of the media by corporations has created a big business-run government and a worthless press leaving Americans screwed and ill-informed.

Adam McKay

The easiest time to be funny is during a fairly serious situation. That way, you can break the ice. It's crazy, but even at funerals, people will get huge laughs.

Adam McKay

The hardest thing in the world to do is to have someone in a seat in a theater laughing so hard that they're making weird sounds.

Adam McKay

The idea of 24-hour news, if you really step back, is pretty insane. Just even saying '24-hour news' almost has satire laced in it.

Adam McKay

The key is a good story. If you have a good story, you have enough emotional beats that you can hit.

Adam McKay

The living nightmare for a red state NASCAR driver would be a gay French driver.

Adam McKay

The stuff that's going on is just so over-the-top, with the banking crisis and destroying the Gulf of Mexico, and the outrage hasn't quite caught up with the people yet. But when it does, I think you're going to see really virulent anti-authoritarian kind of comedy coming out.

Adam McKay

The thing is, I've gotten massages to Enya. I like Enya. If you ate fantastic steaks to Celine Dion, you'd like Celine Dion.

Adam McKay

The truth is, there's an information blockade in America, and it must be broken. In order to find crucial facts, numbers and outside perspectives, a person must spend an hour searching and cross-searching on the computer.

Adam McKay

The way you really stop Al-Qaeda is by stopping their funding. It's not by carpet-bombing or land invasions or anything.

Adam McKay

There are many aspects to directing that have a romantic place in people's minds.

Adam McKay

There's nothing more fun than making fun of what's sacred.

Adam McKay

There's nothing more fun to me than new characters and a new world.

Adam McKay

There's nothing the people love more than a Federal Reserve joke.

Adam McKay

Things I used to get in trouble for writing at 'SNL,' suddenly other people like it.

Adam McKay

Tom Brokaw was never young.

Adam McKay

Ultimately, the only people who are in any way edified by hanging with famous people are you at the age of 11 and your mom.

Adam McKay

Voting for Romney after the train wreck of that was the eight years of W. Bush is like losing your pay check playing a rigged game of three-card monte and then playing the same game again a week later 'cause the cards are a different color.

Adam McKay

Wal-Mart is the biggest distributor of DVDs out there, but personally, I think their manufacturing policies have destroyed our economy, and they don't pay their employees enough. I have massive problems with them.

Adam McKay

We lost our minds in the '80s and '90s; we really as a society just felt that everyone could only care about themselves. There was no responsibility to discuss what's going on in your town, your state, your nation. And it was a blast, it was really fun, but it doesn't work.

Adam McKay

We, Will Ferrell and I, were approached by Sequoia, which is a big financing firm up in Palo Alto; they do a lot of Internet stuff, and they came to us and said they had an idea for a comedy site, and Will and I were sorta like, 'Yeah, we don't know. It's the Internet, we've seen it come and go.'

Adam McKay

When I was at 'SNL,' I would constantly get in arguments, 'Why aren't we more political? We're not going after Bush.' Then look what happened - that Sarah Palin season, they were on fire. It was about something.

Adam McKay

When the movie starts playing on TV and DVD, that's when you really see what the movie is.

Adam McKay

When you do comedy, you get impervious to good and bad reviews.

Adam McKay

White-collar crime has been marketed - billions of dollars have been put in to have us be bored by it.

Adam McKay

With the derivatives market larger than ever, we need way more regulation of Wall Street, not less.

Adam McKay

Word of mouth and the Internet are the only press we have left.

Adam McKay

You can't really do a big character in an action film; you're already suspending your disbelief in the action, then to suspend your disbelief in the character is too much.

Adam McKay

You have a guy like Bernie Madoff literally steal $80 billion, you know, AIG steal hundreds of billions, Goldman Sachs. Crime has changed so much, and to really do a movie with, like, drug dealers or drug smugglers is kind of almost quaint at this point.

Adam McKay

You have to be able to fail with the improv. You have to not care.

Adam McKay

You know how in every heist movie they get past the security cameras that show the hallway leading to the diamonds by jamming the screens with a fake signal of everything looking safe and quiet? Usually a guard coughs so they don't notice the blip from switching to the bogus feed.

Adam McKay

You need the audience to go on the ride with you. You can't just isolate them.

Adam McKay

You think of movies like 'Midnight Run' and '48 Hours', those are great movies, especially 'Midnight Run.'

Adam McKay

You're not a slave to those test audiences.

Adam McKay

This page is intentionally left blank

This page is intentionally left blank

This page is intentionally left blank

This page is intentionally left blank

This page is intentionally left blank

www.ingramcontent.com/pod-product-compliance
Lightning Source LLC
Chambersburg PA
CBHW061929280526
45787CB00004B/1543